One Bent Twig

Tricia Knoll

FUTURECYCLE PRESS
www.futurecycle.org

Cover photo, "Hornbeam leaves"; author photo by Kristin D'Agostino; cover and interior design by Diane Kistner; Adobe Garamond Pro text and titling

Library of Congress Control Number: 2022944715

Published by FutureCycle Press
Athens, Georgia, USA

ISBN 978-1-952593-39-0

To all who plant trees or fight to save old forests.
A special nod to those working to restore American Chestnut
stands and call this Hope.

Contents

Singing whales, talking trees, dancing bees, birds who make art,
fish who navigate, plants who learn and remember.
We are surrounded by intelligences other than our own,
by feathered people and people with leaves. —Robin Wall Kimmerer

The cause of the world's woe is birth,
the cure of the world's woe is a bent stick. —Jack Kerouac

Funeral in the Forest

I mourn, not only for you: all the dying, lies, lynching—
my list is long. But we are here alone, you and I,
and you are gone. I am your wake.

I postponed this ten times, held vigil
on the porch. I had to think about the words
of eulogy, what song, what recognition.

The forester pegged your age at two hundred years
so I assumed you would outlive me, grand sugar maple
with tapping scars, stumps of lost limbs, and brown ridges

of bark twisted to find better rooting, to respond
to your home in this second-growth forest of fox,
black bear and the thick silence of this summer moon.

Two hundred years ago, Thomas Jefferson complained
of a broken wrist while writing a letter to offer to sell
some of his slaves to finance the University of Virginia.

Two hundred years ago, the Missouri Compromise allowed
Missouri to become a state with slaves. Darwin launched
the HMS Beagle. Prospectors discovered gold in Georgia.

You stood here through Abenaki's land claims,
cholera epidemics, Jim Crow, Hurricane Irene.
World wars. Women and the vote. Sap flowed

to syrup. You crashed in that storm a week past.
Wind gusts slashed through your crown of new leaves.
I heard you thunk down beside the ash that fell last fall.

I don't bring music. Below the ledge, we hear coyotes
howl. Mourning doves and hawks. I speak
my litany of loss. I praise that you knew no malice.

You were the forest's lungs. Shade for the sugar man.
The owl's post; the flying squirrel's leap.
What I knew of standing stature in repose.

I wear what seems fit for your last rites—
blue jeans, riding boots, a maple leaf in my hair—
to sit astride you as I would an ancient horse:

the blue dun grullo of cave paintings.
Bareback on your open-air sleep in wildwood
waiting for night to light your yahrzeit fireflies.

My voice? At moonrise, I'll ring the temple bell hung
on the younger maple and bow to the vibrations.
Your lonely place of rest-in-peace. And mine.

I Want to Write

how quaking aspen memorize
    the end rhymes of creation myths

how dance classes for willow branches
    warm up by sleeping beside the mother

what the frail crown
    of a cedar senses when the crow grabs on

the sighs one maple in the sugarbush
    shares with its neighbor

I want to write the prayer winds
    that fan the ginkgo's gold

the sonorous eulogies
    of giant sequoias for each other

how the Bodhi tree knows
    that when it dies another sprouts

how Joshua trees
    smell the Santa Ana winds

I want to write a diary of the bristlecone pine
    from the day humans invented script

I want to write my own life
    one bent twig among many

Touch and Go

First he was only an arm, young skin,
muscles, next to me in a sangha circle.
His tree-of life tattoo, Yggdrasil,
above his wrist, his soft fist,
roots tangled to serve canopy,
canopy arched to feed roots.

He shared a piece of his story.
Single-parent father
of two boys under the age of five.
One whimpered in daycare
while the older balanced maple blocks.

I asked to touch his ink, smooth
black tracery on a white man's skin.
I trace my fingertips on this tree,
following branches on his chest.

Ancient yew, broad counselor
of roots that plunge to center,
home-grounds the eagle,
forms the hard arrow,
tethers the sure-footed stallion
whose hooves seek
the rock cliff's paths
that connect destinies,
and sends squirrel messengers
between twilights of the nine worlds—
doom and joy,
trance and communion,
drum and song.

The Crowhurst Yew

Once I knew that water sang.
Clouds flew on wings.
Trees had doors.
Then I forgot.

My world became
radios and CDs.
Crows on power poles.
Push-buttons.

Maybe it's the dimming
of my eyes, the dulling
of my teeth, how my feet
ache. Being alone.

I turn to simple ways,
knock on that ill-hung door
that opens inward to the yew,
to sit in dark where roots splay,

and ask, *Come back
from the bone yard.*
Beside me, ghost man,
in yew-love this day.

All I Am

I am all that trees know,
even new rot in the oak bole.

I am all that never was
spangled across a maddening sky,

the point on a circle
on the snake's tail and the moon.

I am the half-flutter of a memorial ribbon
tied to an elm, words sunburned away,

or the teacup with the glued-on handle
no one trusts to carry hot water.

I am all that trees forget,
the passing of footsteps.

My Walk-In Museum of Natural History

Please leave your shoes beside my garden clogs by the front door.

Listen for the gong between temporary installations. Today six peacock feathers—five of which are white. Half a robin's egg on the fireplace mantle beside the wind-up tap dance man. A Navajo rug older than you.

Inhale the smell of wet husky and dusty black-and-silver-striped velvet on an over-stuffed loveseat. The reference room features a miniature *Oxford English Dictionary*, a magnifying glass, topographical maps of Oregon's national forests, a slide rule, and a Scrabble dictionary. Enjoy the incense of clove, camphor, and sandalwood.

This museum is a treasury of doors ajar, windows to the woods, and silent solar panels at work. View the collection of Zuni animal fetishes (sorted by creatures of air, land, or sea) made of jet or the swallowtail butterfly pinned in a Lucite box.

What I don't point out is the vase of roses from a new hybrid, fluttery blooms with the subtlety of silk and a dusting of cocoa on petals that frame a molten center. Those who notice them will find their shoes wiped clean of mud and filled with peppermints when it is time to go.

If you walk to the creek to view the fire-scarred cedar root wad, you may pick a fig or sit below the vine maple on a bench next to Garden Buddha. This is where the museum opens its vault. Green meets sky.

> holy joy also
> filters
> through fissures

You Never Forget the First Trees You Love

You hid in oak shade to practice
air guitar to escape the diva's aria
over-rehearsed in the dining room.

You used branches to climb higher
than authorities said you could
for the silence of the ash confessional.

When a tornado turned the air
sick green, you mourned lost limbs,
realized steadfastness has a cost.

You hoarded acorn skulls
with straight faces and ruffled berets
to throw at your brothers

and made battle lines
behind horse chestnuts and crabapples.
You squatted on surface roots for rest.

These friends' generous kin
embrace in green wherevers,
forest clans.

Predator Eyes

We are groomed to watch pages turn
in the storybooks Grandma shares

about woozle tracks, nuns on parade,
Quidditch, Babar's escape, ducklings,

and the manners of walking sticks.
To follow what moves. Bison, pheasant,

Road Runner cartoons, horse races, Roller Derby,
tightrope walkers, and Alderaan cruisers.

When clouds trundle and shuffle over picnics
above the ticklish grass we imagine

a bulbous nose that morphs to hay wain,
filigrees of fences that smear

to washes of mile-long horsetails
to thin blankets that invite a nap.

We count the hours to rain
as shadows slide over cornfields.

From the deathbed the soul
rises, seeks an open window.

The hunter's sharp-eye focus
has more to do than study nudes

of trees that drop their leaf shawls,
witness their forked fates, seek limb-truth

in the way the trees mirror the meanders
of rivers toward deltas.

Slow goes unnoticed
as it grows older than the hunter.

Nurse Log

When we lie down in death

do we invite children
to spring up from our bellies?

To sink through us
to the water table?

To outshine us
in our stupor?

Do we nourish them
with plan or happenstance?

Or hold them to the light?

Fig Tree

Naomi says her father
never told a story
without including a fig tree.

A donkey tied to a tree trunk
or brothers who pass one
as they quarrel.

The muscular fig
roots beyond its limbs,
slurps most of the garden water,

the habit of a good story.
Although it's hard to hide a fig tree,
I discovered mine late.

Nightshade, morning glory,
honeysuckle and alder shoots
threw a green cloak cover.

I clawed off stranglers,
booed at the squirrels,
and finding it,

it found me, fig girl
whose story seems as short
as the shelf-life of a fig.

Solace

Jerry saw the silhouette of his father's face
in the naked branches of the oak tree.
That was how he knew he could cry,
that his father would be at hand
at least through this winter, his father
who took him up the hill to the park
to see dragons and tractors in storm clouds.

His brother brought pepperoni pizza,
not enough for the retired teachers
and suburban friends who showed up
with deviled eggs and focaccia sandwiches
or the aging men with motorcycles drinking
beer down the street. His neighbor Lou
was kind enough to say he saw the face
even though he insisted those arriving
should park their cars inside the lines
and not leave the doors hanging open
while they unbuckled children and hugged
as if they hadn't seen their cousins
three weeks ago at the ninetieth
birthday party where the now-dead
patriarch had praised the frosted green cake
for his Irish wife he said he planned
to see again soon. That night he blew
out nine wavering candles with such vigor
that Jerry thought he might live
forever or at least to ninety-one.

Now that face in limbs. Jerry stands
on the curb, looks west where sunset
backlights the oak. The laughing lip is right,
the add-on tuft of scraggle beard. At midnight
Jerry decides to remain silent about the likeness
hovering in that tornado-twisted oak.
No one expects Jerry to nurture the family
as his father did with stories mixing truth
and hyperbole, humor and righteousness.
It was enough to not be left alone.

Faith

I am not the rib-bone
of an apple-chomping Adam.

The smell of apple blossom
promises pies and peels.

I do not fear snakes.
I wear no sackcloth

bindings, white robes,
or a cross on a bronze chain.

I clap with two hands
and know one tree hears

when another falls.
My toes root,

tickle up mushrooms,
and curl into leaf fall.

I don't confuse wind-song
with choirs of angels.

I Look for a Harbinger of Hope

It might be tattered clouds pulling back.
Full moon on this night when rivers flood,
cars float at crosswalks, gutters back up, roofs leak.
The visible moon after weeks of rain
and slush. Or one star above the alder. A lamp.

Slumped from a meeting about democratic process
on this warmed-up night that mixes sleet
and snowmelt into treachery, it might be glancing
into the coffee shop steamed from latte-making.
A couple sits near the window seriously together. A love.

My car is parked under a naked tree of wicked sticks
balancing in limbs from the blow-downs. A car waits
down the block at a stop sign, headlights
on wet pavement, slick black without streetlights.
Loose-joint trot in front of the car. A coyote.

The Tale End of the Monsoon after Reading Hanshan

My toe-push lifts the oak rockers, here
where I want to be, snuggled out of gale winds
that plagued his road to Cold Mountain—

that tree-top mist, wet stones, fishtail-slapping
streams, hidden caves and well-strung vines,
gusts that nabbed the climber's breath
and flipped his scholar's pages toward death.

By my fire, my old-woman shadow
slips back and forth in bedrock dark
into a vision of his papers stuffed
beneath the roots of roots to keep them dry.

My window opens to a swirl of branches writhing
and leaves all brouhaha, what he kept at bay
hunkered beneath a cinnamon tree.

Stick Figures

In June they stood full-fledged righteous,
  sober and breeze-bluffed dancing.

Now maples as bare bones, articulated
  witnesses to the blows of winter wind.

At their feet, cast-off blouses, skirts and veils—crumpled
  summer, last landings of a headband of leaves

tinted saffron and orange, turmeric and sumac, cayenne,
  fenugreek and ginger, mace, sage and cinnamon.

While first-grade twins draw members holding hands,
  these figures grow go-betweens in firmaments of dirt

and hold forth in sagging winter shawls, hijabs
  and turbans of snow under a horned moon,

expectant even unto the crackle glaze of ice.

Birch Bark

*I have heard of a man in Maine who copied the whole
Bible onto birch bark.* —Henry David Thoreau

Before I knew what Thoreau wrote
I sent you a letter from the dogs
written on birch bark that asked
you to sniff it to know where
they had been, how they wished
you were there.

It must have been like that
for that man. Distilling:

Be kind.
Keep in mind
how hard that is,
but relish
the journey.
Ignore what is false.
Smell the birch
to remember sweet.
Bend it into a canoe
when you must
get away.

Those Christmas Trees

1

Underneath, swaddled in a bunting
in a basket, I stared up at porcelain angels
amid red and green lights in tin-foil stars.

2

My father walked me down the stairs
with a towel over my eyes into the kitchen
so I'd eat before I saw what was under the tree:
a three-speed red bike with hand brakes,
the lights I saw before the bike.

3

In Girl Scouts we made ornaments from tin can lids
and glitter or clothespins painted with eyes
and glued-on red-cotton Rudolph noses.

4

The footprint of my one-year-old daughter
stamped in blue tempera paint on pink paper.
Its green-and-white ribbon loop fastens
to the tree with a photo of her reluctance to get messy.

5

A potted fir for my mother dying
of cancer and its wee wooden figures—
a woodsman hauls a tree, a caroler
holds a golden song book, a blue angel
plays a flute, and a cardinal sits at a feeder.

6

My friends take a narrow box
from the closet, shake out
a wired tree and plug it in.

7

The deaf man down the road
grows four-foot trees on two urban lots.
Special for seniors: $12 for a fir
with no limbs on the bottom two feet.

8

I ship old ornaments
to my daughter in Vermont—
German glass, the apple
with a skater inside waltzing
on a mirror, the moose on a roof.
I save dozens of gold birds
on clips, a few missing tail feathers,
and that flimsy footprint.

9

My decoration collection shrinks
to two shoe boxes. I give away
strands of blue lights. My next tree
may be no bigger than my mother's,
dressed in nothing but tiny birds.

Additions to the Understory

*...to / you and your children: // stay together / learn
the flowers / go light* —Gary Snyder

Shade and shadow aren't the sum of it
as vine maple reaches for direct sun
within constraints of summer's canopy.

Nor totals of little lives, the ants' den
and their linear scurry of eggs.
Or overlooked adventures of beetles

while fungi diligently does its work
of decay and the ensantina salamanders
seek damp camouflage in rotten logs.

What was the motive behind the flurry
of paper in the hands of a woman I saw
from my window one Saturday morning?

She stood in the rain at my poetry box
and shuffled forty poems to choose one.
Her understory I learn later

when I meet her at the box
in the Saturday drizzle
with a new poem to post.

Firm paper going limp. She sobs.
Her sixteen-year-old son died
on that first Saturday morning.

She is back for another poem.
I offer the one I hold, unknowing,
Gary Snyders's "For the Children."

The canopy stretches. Secrets, saplings,
snakes, beings of our understories,
hear mosquito whines

and tree frogs that cling
to branches with their feet
as leaves start adding up.

Tree Ghost

This morning a tossed-off plastic bag snags
high in a red oak, a tug-of-war chuffing kite.

What if I cat-climbed,
stuffed this flimsy ghost with weights
unfit for my pockets

       mother's apron strings
       key to the blue house
       the twenty-five-cent milk tooth
       Ares and Scorpio wedding rings
       letters from the man I left
       that coarse black braid hacked off
           before her hair fell out

and begged for breeze
to blast that bag
out of my hoarding hands?

Lichen Through the Lens

Fall's twilight sifts down
through ponderosas and junipers.
We, young boy and crone, amble
through kicked-up dust, fire-scarred pines,
whiskered lupines shrunk to dry pods,
and count ground squirrel holes under snags.

You snap off a fistful of lichen, pot-scrubber
in neon green, grizzled old man's beard
on a dead twig. *Lichen,* I say, *probably fungi.*
You say *My teacher said fungi is bad.*
No! I come back, too loud for dimming-down day
thinking wine, cheese, penicillin, root symbiosis;
you think ringworm, comic monsters.
We focus my magnifying lens on the grizzle.
How do we tell good from bad?

The internet sleeping in our dark cabin
wakes to *Letharia columbiana,*
brown-eyed wolf lichen.
People here before fence posts
dyed their dancing blankets
in this spiky tangle
that can poison wolves.

You line up a kitchen-table battlefield
of plastic men in armor
who ambush angry dragons
from your wolf-lichen lairs.

I window-watch for stars
over juniper and wish you
and all wolves well.

A Radio Quiz

It starts with a word choice,
rough or *smooth*?
I choose *rough*.

Weathered barn doors,
goat hair, cedar bark,
lava rock, and tea rose thorns.

Stop! The Pacific Madrona
peels of bark sheets to all-bare
red-brown, the for-no-other

reason than smooth,
a peel to the core
like sudden love

on a rain-drenched afternoon.

Ready to Walk

The deepest-rooted dream of a tree is to walk…
—Joy Harjo

My friend said the red maple outside her window
wanted to walk to the riverbank. *Because it leans?*
I asked. *No, in my midnight dream, a rain noise,
the tree at the river, where it wants to be.*

She was counting her end days or, more precisely,
we were counting, staring outside with her.
We agreed to let that tree walk, untethered
as she imagined while her life wound down.

If this were one of our kitchen-talk days,
I might have asked if being rooted
is that tree's power. Living thoroughly where
you are born? Knowing home abides

at the molecular level? To grant whims
to wind and snow. Sunbathe.
Yield. Flinch and persevere,
earth as homestead.

Her death would be
a *walking on,* she insisted.
Later I saw her through death's door
left ajar for her to go,

grateful the tree stayed put.

Newly Discovered Hole

My tiny terrier digs at the base of the tree
I call mine. How much damage can her claws
do to this cedar, some hundred years standing?
I lean over the hole she explores to test
how deep the tunnel goes. Wrist deep.
Her eyebrows arch in *I-told-you-so.*

Four women friends have lamented
that a park employee removed
the frilly fairy doors and windows
two artists installed in tree nooks
in Maricara Nature Park.
I hope my tree invites
homeless fairies to sanctuary.

I line up six gray river rocks
near the opening.
I sense a shadow.
Stones at the cave? Or entrance
stelae for woodsy creatures
with feet the size of pinpricks?

Bark, I tell the terrier,
if fairies grab your toes.
Come get me if the stones roll away.

The Woods with No Name

Coffee spurs my attempt to think of news items
as stones I can shake through a screen
to separate pea gravel from golf balls.
The pope reflects on climate change.
A man running for Congress assaults a reporter.
Bells toll in Manchester. The children march.
All the rocks stay upside the screen. Big deals.

I go out to the woods with no name
to meet again breezes, fog drip, old firs,
and a few tall weeds. Perhaps to prune
that overgrown white camellia
whose brown blooms litter the ground.
Dead twigs clutter its innards.

I think in visuals—to open a sight line
to the obelisk raised for a dead son. Gut
what is dead or yellowed. Lift what bows.

When I finish, a shapely shrub stands
on the verge of these woods with no name.
Pruned so delicately no one will ask
Who did that? How did this happen?

Star Chart

Each stump bears a ring cycle.
Years of fat or lean, dry or green,
a few under attack.

Draw the rings of your heartwood.
Color each circle in a hue
to soothe you.

Sketch tight lines for years you forget,
your bark of early memories—
swimming in the lake with alewives.

Shade under the napping crabapple.
The car with a clutch that you drove away
from home. That summer locusts erupted.

Make concentric circles of your sequences.
Swellings for tragedies or pregnancies
when a burl bulged.

Pin up this wavering star chart, a bull's-eye,
to an oak in the skyscraper woods
where your grandchildren play hide and seek.

The Saw Cut of the Downed Red Cedar in Tryon Creek State Park

To count the thirty-seven rings on this tree body
eight times longer than mine, I kneel on a trail
beneath dappling vine maples.

That many years ago,
my daughter learned to walk.
I changed jobs and bought a home

when this tree-corpse sprouted.
Its heartwood refuses to dent
under my fingernail.

A slug the color of army fatigues
lifts to slide up from the duff
to climb the saw-cut.

The slug is as wide as a pencil,
the length of my ring finger.
Its tentacles tilt right / then left

as it secretes enough slime
that a blade of grass hitches a ride up
from the understory of duckfoot.

By the time I hoist myself to return to the bridge,
the slug has glided thirty-seven years.
Time moving like mine.

Six Chanticleer Pears on NE 27th

Yesterday I drove by those Chanticleers
I planted in front of that brown bungalow,
my home for twenty years. Good street trees
in a solid neighborhood, they've grown three stories,
got hacked open mid-canopy for power lines,
survived ice-torn limbs and truck-scrape tattoos,
to thrive to bloom fairy-teacup blossoms
that don't bear fruit.

I had no placentas to line the holes
for those champagne-flutes of pear trees.
We tucked each in with one poem
under the root ball—an old sestet
about those who plant a tree
never knowing who lives the longest.

My hysterectomy trees I call them,
planted for a lost womb. I cajoled
a young couple and an ex-cop
to join me to make blooms and shade
for our alternately sun-fried,
freeze-dried street.

Galloping Hooves

The grain of a wood is the language of a tree.
—Ursula K. Le Guin

I have an oak desk
and a zelkova sewing box.
They hold their tongues today.

So too the oak fireplace mantle.
Fir picture frames and pastry boards.
That cherry spoon a cousin carved.
A ruler from grade-school.

Quiet script on the oak desk
shows growth rings that sucked water,
how the carpenter lined up joins
so that end grains trace
flecks of music notes.

Then, those time signatures
in the nicks from hooves
of black metal stallions I galloped
on the dark mahogany
dining room table burnt
umber from a prairie sun.

For what we never said
at that table fifty years ago—
I pick up a soft rag
and beeswax paste,
rub the tight grain
to lay to rest
what I might have said.

Sewing Box

Made in Japan circa 1880

A woman asked for this box—
with a slot for a measuring stick,
a built-in pin cushion, four drawers
and a cubby to store needles and threads.

Did she choose the zelkova wood
or did the cabinetmaker believe
these pieces with bold ripples
and gold whorls were best?

Why did she sell it?
Maybe she died.

                    *

My first husband found it
forty years ago in an Oriental
antique shop. His gift for me,
she who never sews.

The inside smells like lemons
and old drought. Drawers hold
jangle-tags from my first dog,
a one-pocket purse of green silk.
Tarot cards, a retirement medallion,
the porcelain cat my friend left me.

For that seamstress in Japan,
I tuck inside a brass thimble
full of blue-corn flour, Zuni staple
to fuel long journeys.

A polished hand-me-down
for my daughter to hold
to its two-hundredth year.

Name the Dread

1

A fear of falling into the sky has a name,
but not the dread that sky may fall on you.

A prophesy for Aeschylus said something falling
would kill him. He believed in oracles.

He sat only in sunshine, away from shadows,
buildings, and heavy-limbed trees.

Then—the day an eagle flew over
his bald head, thought his scalp a rock

and dropped a turtle from its talons
to smash the shell on a shining boulder.

Death-by-turtle-fall for this tragedian who said
and now it goes as it goes and where it ends is Fate.

2

Falling skies in Syria, Iraq, Afghanistan, Hiroshima
and Nagasaki pound out booms louder than thunder,

sun-ups brighter than lightning. If the fear of all bombs
has no name, bombs do—Grand Slam. The Mother of All

Bombs is so big she requires her own cargo plane.
The Massive Ordnance Penetrator (MOP).

Little Boy. Fat Boy. Someone other than poets
and priests choose these *noms de guerre.*

3

An ecology teacher walked in Oxbow Park in January
beside her fiancé in a light wind by the Sandy River.

A cottonwood twitched, toppled, trapped her,
killed her. Two-hundred silent teens came

to her open-casket funeral to say good-bye,
for many their first death.

In a flowered skirt, her mother hunched
on a stool beside the bier to read a story

that ends *Good night noises everywhere.*
This name, grief.

In the Shadow of the Hanging Tree at Ghost Ranch

Our poetry class lingers in the stretched shade of this hanging tree
where a dozen decades ago a rustler-murderer was lynched.
Scars on this cottonwood at the height of my heart
tell of dropped limbs, weight and time.
My teacher reads Rilke:
You must change your life.

Was it a night noose, that dark dangling
strangle that let his wife and child flee
to the reservation? Did the judge
cut down the dead bad man
like the witch who opens
her oven door—with caution?

This hanging tree forgets
dirges when dying is done,
sustains a violin and cello duet
with sunset's purple haze that invites
deer to sneak by.

Its bark braids like dry arroyos
and it drops gold switches that children
flick to slap their thighs, that the lover
lifts in humor to bless the head of his beloved.
A hole near the roots shows rot.

In late-in-the-day shadow-cast of this witness tree,
I lean back, share Basho's simple sentence:
Come see the true flowers of this pained world.

California Sycamore

You are a she, not an it, a tree that highnesses over me
sixty slender graces tall. Three trunks from one root mass
that crawl with black ants announce wind's betrayal
and pruning saws. Your roots clutch a granite boulder
thicker than my waist.

You, Amazon beside a rush-down creek. Inside a forest
of other matrons, your bulk signals presence.
I touch your skin, gray on weathered ivory,
a pattern that fawns mimic to hide in littered leaves, blotches
on uniforms for soldiers in desert wars.

You do not rest easy here.
Too many right-angles speak of conflict.
One upper snake-branch withers dead.
Yes, yearn toward the water, lean to thrive.

Then the scar where you lost a fourth trunk,
a limb that leaned too far. A wind challenge
years ago. You responded to this unkind loss,
secreting an oval scab the color of blood-clot.

This. Your vulva, my dear, a burlish blackness
so like the slit of women. I compare the roughness
to the sleek silver sheen above.
Within your scar tissue I find the twist
of an owl's face, night hunger of the raptor.

Around the slash you extruded bulges
of swollen labia. Cellular swelling to violation.
You sprout months-old twigs on your sun-side base.
She who serves to shade in silence. So often this
is the whole sad, sordid, resilient test
that faces the women of the world.

The Tree of Long Life Is Kindling

From "Old Dust" by Li Po

As to firing clay, beside the raku kiln
wait fibers of rush, wet leaves, brush for reducing.

As the breath of the dragon that the ancients drew
scorches a cave or forces sky-play of wind-sore clouds
at sunset. Pyres by the river. Bonfires
spook flimsy ash that twists into vapor.

Sere splints at the torch
ignite gratitude. This, now—
no matter which way
flames leap.

1950s Dragon Breath

Scritch of metal tines on concrete called
our gang from the fort in the woods.
We abandoned paint-can seats,
acorn cups and mushroom-rotted logs.

Fathers in padded jackets and duckbill hats
raked oak leaves in low October sun. Scritch
of rake—we brought twigs to burn
as fathers whooshed up fire with a little gas

and much damp smoke and shifted us
from one side to the other as the wind eddied.
No one mentioned air pollution, climate change
or carbon sequestration. This was ritual,

our pretend cook fires on the oxbow of the Platte,
banks of dry waving grasses, tribes circled.
Smoke trending to pale. From the crackling
of a burn pile, this taut smell was fall

going toward Halloween and shorter days.
Liquid fire tongues leapt. If the men
talked politics, we didn't listen.
They broomed strays toward the bonfire.

If this was a playdate, we didn't know it.
If the future would yield up yard debris bins,
we were too deep in rites of fire to imagine them.
When the heaps were ash, we ran

back to our fort, sugared up
on ashy marshmallows,
a wild smell of char in our hair,
that replaced new-mowed lawns.

We'd seen the dragon,
heard it cackle, and expected fall
would always be the same.
Fathers. Rakes. Fire.

Through Flames in the New Year's Fire

Winter, Last

In the middle of the forsythia,
bare limbs snagged remnant spider strands
beaded with raindrops.

There were accidents. That grandma in the emergency room
believed she was seated on an oak pew in church
until she peed her pants.

Greens—neon moss backed the synagogue cornerstone steps
to the sanctuary where the folksinger's casket rested on a bier.

An ad in the *New York Times*
announced new zombie books
to ship on Valentine's Day.

Icicles hung like fiendish teeth.

Spring

Snowdrops first.

The ornithologist explains his diagnosis,
his fingers flutter
over the rose coverlet on his bed.
He says it will rain soon.
We can see the sleet.

In the damp cardboard box packed with teacups,
one dry spider curled in yellow newspaper from 1992.

In the barn, piles of horse hair
blow into corners of drafty stalls.
Two mice molded in hayloft traps.

Summer

Ripe peach skin
hid the rugged terrain of pits.

To transplant pearly everlastings for the bees,
I tugged apart thick, tangled roots.

The third-grade teacher died after Alzheimer's.
Her daughter set out red candles, red geraniums
and a photo from her best and second marriage.
The speakers played Navajo flute songs.

Fall

One pencil-thin stem of a white rose held on to one brown leaf.
Maple leaves studded the sidewalk with red stars.
I saw no night stars during four weeks of fog.

Professor "Bird Man" died.
I drove 95 miles from a poetry reading
to the century-old red barn for his tribute,
wore the same gray-and-black-striped dress to both.

Tacked to the wall of the barn—
a dusty red second-place ribbon
from a horse show in 1998.

Winter, This

The forecast shouts out *polar vortex.*

My fire in logs of compressed wood chips
sputters on the bed of raked ash. I eat
a pomegranate, red food for the dead.

I redeem a gift certificate at Powell's Books.
From a poetry shelf, nesting side by side,
birth, love, aging and death. I choose Bly.

I sip a mellow Brunello.
My fingers massage the gutter of the book.
I touch the words nearby: *prepared for death.*

Windfire Smoke from Northern Forests

Not just hills obscured behind a thin skim
or sunsets ignited like flames of forges.
Not the crackled whine of trees going gone,
or soot stinks that bed into sheets on the line.

Think photos of cities we thought were China.
Thick drifts of smudge that share nothing
with mist. Summer grief that turns the clock
back to zero on that regrowth plot of trees.

The new parents worry about the lungs
of a newborn boy named for a mountain.
The sting of red eyes, ash on a tongue
that licks lips like an eel entering a trap.

The flailing gray ghost's promise—
this begins what happens next.

Tenpenny Hammered

Stand straight and sober
to your cross-hatched hat.

Yours is no gummy playground
like the toothpick's.

Slump and you're as dead
as rust and sawdust,

victim of the claw end.
Embrace your smell of oil,

you wanna-be in the paper bag,
five-facets to the point.

Forget your dream
of gouging into bark

with lovers' initials.
They found a better tool.

Fingers that cannot hold water
slam the hammer's wrath-whack

to your head. Be the needle
of joineries. Wed the woods.

Your ode reads
when the cabin burns,

rake nails from the ash.
Only in burial

are you of use to anyone.

Salad Days

A linguist bemoans the disuse of these two words.

In by-gone days I was frilly endive, earnest
to be crunch-lush. Then a mate presented himself
as a creative carrot offering rosebud radishes.

We once ignored parents who snuggled
like faded packages of eggplant seeds
in kitchen drawers. Ignorant that widows
might wear perennial weeds.

We did not wilt. Or slime in a fridge.
We took on kale and beets,
menus for chops, Cobbs,
Caesars, and romaines
yet came to relish
winter-over longevities:
parsley and pickles.

We age more like trees.
Patient. Unconcerned
with forked appearances.
Happy to have a bird alight.
Hours of the oak.

Walking into the Shadows of Ashford Forest

This high grove is a forest the old know, above the torii gate
beyond Esquiver River and Wolf Creek. Below, the young
saw up woodlots for timber. I pass stumps, leave behind
papered-over windows, the glare of streetlights,
patched storefront flags, and concrete outposts.

These woods hide markers. A maple burl grew
around a brass bell. Black rocks bear the singe
of fire-song rings. There's a spring, the moss-silenced
falls, one beeswax candle stub, a tribe of armless
porcelain Charlotte dolls copper-wired to limber twigs.
The fir-green of promises and prayer.

My Thunderbird slippers soften my sore soles.
I knead my toes, dip them in the rill. An aging woman
sways like wands of brittle birch. A bit stiff,
a little lithe, wind-bent, stilling to sit
on stone outcrops above the maze of worms.

My simple needs—a willow basket, two bits of bone,
a scrape of mother's cliff-blown ash, that packet
of dried huckleberries. A stirring scapula
of driftwood marks where I suspect this trail ends,
where the shivering found shelter decades ago.

This is a place to lay down life. No sizzle.
No rectangular caskets. I find the curved eagle wing
carved into Feather Rock, hear the fan
of ravens on wing lift. Read the print of deer,
the scrapes of black bear, and the withering of blackberry
bramble. Reach for moonlit flakes of an early snow.

My body goes to ground in the well of a fir,
a tent of bending branches. I count holy star-fire,
see a glory of holes in the night, and press
my down-going breast,
into this day of intimate clay.

Brown

I live with brown hair,
floozied up, fine mahogany
inlaid with gold.
Or, less sure, thin
and mousy.

I envy friends who've lost brown,
alchemy to hand-wrought sterling silver
locks or dry, settled ash
of down-sized driftwood fires—
hair grandchildren understand
as Grandma's arms circle hugs
and she plays games of on-and-off
the train or make a cave.

Of the two, the silver and the brown,
I end with both, rooted in redeeming
loam, rotted fir needles and cedar boughs,
dirt that tastes like all life in a finger lick,
smells like rain a worm has known.
No boxes or death wrap shrouds.

Scoop me from the pyre's ash.
Tender me to soil
near this creek's meander
through the duff of oak.

Echo

The widow names the copper beech Echo,
scratches that returning word on bark
to mark where her walk turns around
at its shade and her golden retriever's
meditations on roots.

Which, she asks, is more honest:
lover's initials scraped in exposed sand
at low tide or a knife scar on a tree trunk?
One submits to wave, the other lasts
beyond love and the chiseler's hand.

She sees a green man's face in this beech's
burls and branches, eyes at the pruning
place, nostrils at the nodes, and beards
in shedding bark. She asks of each beech,
the willow with its gold skirts,
even the marcescent oak:

If you wrote on my skin in a sway of wind,
what would your leafy brushstrokes
spell?

Stripes

Stripes run away toward infinity—
raspberry rows, beach towels and barbed-wire fences,
stones at veteran cemeteries, shirts on jockeys,
whip-flay scars on a winced back.

In those places where engineers offer
parallels and planes, staircases, highway lines,
when poets write left to right or right to left
or up to down to fence-board meaning,

you could show off stripes you earned—
boy scout, firefighter, officer, security—
as if they are contrails on a mission
or barcodes of best.

The children practice script and subtraction
for gold stickers that may fall off their papers
or for the teacher's scrawl of five-line stars
as they sit in rows of desks and walk in lines.

Think striped creatures. Of course, zebras.
Slugs, skinks, skunks, tabbies and tigers,
mice, chipmunks, numbats and nyalas.
okapi and angelfish. Garter snakes.

Me? I ache for pinnate—heavenly bamboo,
the tree of silk, oak and red alder,
maple and peach. Lines that guide the bee.
My camouflage of wrinkles is dendritic.

I step out of line.
Aging does that.

Tree Frogs of North Ash Creek

Portland, Oregon

I listen. Every January night. No mating calls.
The little green *Hyla regilla* are gone from this drainage.
Neighbors sleep without waking.
My bit of world is drop-dead silent.

I wonder where they got to.

Maybe to the vaulted log cathedral where pins drop and all who
listen hear. Where they run into end-of-the-line typewriter bells,
my mother's humming, evening taps at Girl Scout camp, the
slamming door of my father's Buick announcing he came home
from work, Bella's purr like fine gravel in an orange juice can.

Anthology of Stories Told Over Dinner

The daughter says that in Tasmania the peat is burning
for the first time in history.

The uncle tells that in Gallup there was much less snow
than when he came there as a doctor five decades ago.

The ice-out clock drops through the ice on the Vermont pond
a week earlier than when he was a child.

The apple trees put forth buds twenty days early.

The conquistadors rode through New Mexico
and grass grew thigh-high. Now the land burns
and chili peppers suffer from both heat and hail.

Grandfather tells of reading a picture book to his grandson,
one about Santa delivering gifts from a red-and-white-striped boat
with sails made of hemp.

The mother, wiping her hands on a blue cotton apron, pauses
at the kitchen door. *I saw an eagle yesterday. Over the nature area.*

The uncle solicits money for condor recovery. An amount
equal to the estimated cost of dinner. They pony up.

Other stories they might have told stop
with arrival of rhubarb pie. The sun sets

on an urban creek where there are no longer any frogs.

My Bonsai Tree on the Southern Window Ledge in the Laundry Room

To the nearly four-hundred-year-old Yamaki white pine bonsai that survived the atomic blast in Hiroshima and now lives in an arboretum museum in Washington, DC

This small juniper. Its clay pot
awash in moss weathered for five springs
below my garden Buddha. To take on
another green life gives me pause.

Think first. With each tender snip,
practice what is skillful, kind.
A twig gone. A fraction
of a branch.

Can I be here day-to-day with water
through Augusts of certain drought
to drizzle rituals of commitment?
See it as if it lives on a mountain top?

Tiny: lady bugs at winter's window,
Mom's brass thimble inlaid
with delftware of turning windmills,
and my green cat's-eye marble. Some rationale

for miniatures, a silhouette of relief when our globe
withers with wild viruses or a Yemeni girl
dies of cholera in a flapping tent. This twisted juniper,
its spare shadow laid across the washroom shelf.

Respect for Elders

A tree takes one hundred years or more
to find its *kodama* spirit. Long enough

to outlive the woodsman, prove
resilient to change, go deep

and earn itself a name.

Australia's Tāne Mahuta, Lord of the Forest,
a kauri-tree child of earth and sky.

California's General Sherman, the bulkiest sequoia
and a second, General Lee, for warriors.

Hyperion, the hidden sequoia, the tallest tree
on Earth. Titan.

Cloning, quaking aspen. The Pando
named for *I spread.*

Bristlecone pine and banyan,
the pregnant baobab.

Names for high and wide,
old and tattered.

Seed bearers.
Bud bursters.

The name for my cedar
in these summers of hotter

dryer spells, Old Mother,
the being I water

as wildfire
cremates her kin.

Open Spaces on the Universe's Altar

Measure not with miles, meters, finger widths, rods,
nor hourglasses, stopwatches, plastic kitchen clocks.

Yield to reveries that fly beyond the moon.
Observe your tides of emptiness and breath.

Praise see-beyonds like windowpanes, mirrors,
chalice glass, and prisms casting rainbows.

Your brain tickles you from across a continent.
A phone chimes. Accept that you must answer.

Explore parallels between parent and child
as diablo gusts twist the spiral bonds.

Float with your spirit buoys
on whitecaps nursed in dreams.

Your heart knows why people believe in ether,
listen to trees, stare into the stone bowl's water.

Put aside your fear of black holes. Love old ladies
who reminisce about darning socks

on their front porches
to watch the fall progress

gold leaf by solemn gold leaf.

How to Swear

Many targets for swearing roam this collapsing world. Fouled
places. Obscene weapons. The pandemic. Any predictable,
capricious or even seductive god would damn them. Damn: an
all-purpose recrimination stocked like baking powder and salt.
The only French swear word I know after five years studying this
romance language is *merde,* no relation to murder, more recall of
run-over skunk.

When you abandon your broken-down sedan to the crusher, kick
the flat tire. Or wish for the lover who deserts you to itch eternally.
Do not go commonplace into today's culture of curse.

The voiceless have choices—spray paint, fist shake, march en masse,
and flatulence. Silence is a creative option under the competition of
talk shows, chain saws, leaf blowers, whining tires, and monologues
from dogs trapped on porches. *Merde* under its breath.

Grief's varietal vocabulary includes elephants who boom over
their dead. Whales under sea-roads. A spotted owl's *hup hoo hoo.*
The brash eloquence of the crow. The last stand of the great stand
of sequoias.

Loud gets attention. Newborns know this, but too-long stillness
in a crib also brings tenders running.

Some say climate change is a deserved curse. Changing winds
bring tornadoes that lift roofs and leave the family Bible open on
the kitchen table or rend the Bible and leave the TV guide on the
Tibetan green silk carpet. After one masters swearing or demeaning
(Cyrano's monologue after the viscount), the second lesson—which
requires more finesse and as much sincerity—is blessing.

How to Bless

In Old English etymology, the word "blessing" began with
sprinkling blood on a pagan altar—a hint of messy demands.
The heart requires lessons to learn the way of it. Quiet thankfulness
floats by faster than a cloud of malaise. Ecstasy is not a call to
action. Blessing is an act of volition.

Reliability and consistency are clues to how to invoke blessing.
A second-hand station wagon with a dented door that drives fine.
The seatbelts work. The sonnet that holds up to five readings.
Friends who show up.

Watch for disguised blessings. The messiness of the magnolia.
A robust woman with a veil over scars. The lemon smell of the gold
rose. An extended wait for the diagnosis that nothing is wrong.
Death offering escape.

Yesterday, browned-out moss on the labyrinth greened up after a
shower—not a rain that ended drought—drizzle that changed the
color of things. That sound. Blood on the pagan altar.

Tree Sentiency in Six Thousand Languages

The six thousand tongues of living languages
lap in the wind with words for trees—stand,
forest, tribe, jungle, grove, thicket,
family, weald, woodland—and still
we haven't said it all or anything close
to how trees hold fall's flames,
run spring sap, bloom shoots
in duff, root near shrines,
invite fungi to mediate
between soil and root, cleanse
waste from air, bind the trail,
preserve life and tie fruits to roots.

Their language is not mute, but silent
against hypocrisy, treachery, and
censorship.

Wind exercises the forest's crotches, forks,
arms, and crowns. Sweat moves
in sapwood. Heartwood fights decay.
The tree endures grafting,
the hugging of a vine,
the boring of insects,
inquisitions of birds, and
smotherings of avalanche.

The young seek crevices
in stone walls or beneath pavement
that decades later will heave up
as roots writhe, eating soil.

A family of old-growth, the evergreen
wildness we half-remember like dreams
from yesterday, forgotten patience
as we move away.

What to Expect

The overture hints at the action
of this Opera of the Vanished—
wingbeats of flushed birds, thrum
and buzz of equatorial forests.
Slow resolve. Silence.

A tattered curtain draws open.
Admire spectacle costumes—
parade of show-off
Tasmanian tiger prints.
Wings. Scales. Tails.
Red. Green. Gold. Tawny.

The jester wears trash-can-lid
ears, reminds you this story
is real, invites you to join
a sing-song good-bye.
The libretto becomes disjointed—
words almost recognizable,
like the babble of a worried baby.

He conducts in agile hijinx:
the choir's frog chirrups.
Howls. The violins'
bumblebee flights, and
insect hums never named.
Piccolo birds. His recitative
behind a gong's echo
names those on parade. Some
will sing of shrouded deaths
more opaque than murder.

Finale: backdrop habitats collapse,
Amazon folds on top of ocean-scape.
The lost wander in low-lying fog
like waves, row upon row.
One aria of *om,* melismatic
moaning glaciers. Surround-sound.

The overture repeats. Beings retreat
to blackout. Curtains close.
The jester demands this: *No clapping.*

The Seven Gourd Works Project

For Iain Woodhouse

The Seven Gourd Works began in a computer lab. A scientist
erased trees, airbrushed Constable, Seurat, and Van Gogh to
scorched earth, scrubbed the world's best breath away one oak
at a time, a pine, then olives and mulberries.

In Ohio, an artist scoops oxide sludge below an abandoned coal
mine and stirs it into paint. Red, orange, yellow, green, blue,
indigo, violet toxic rainbows.

In Beijing cellists tie on white masks to perform a symphony of
coal smog shadows. An oboist wears a bowtie the color of soot.

A rich man on the mountain hears of these. He buys a woodblock
print celebrating passenger pigeons. He listens to recordings of
crosscuts of tree rings played on a record player. He hums a song
about yellow taxis.

He funds the Seven Gourd Works, castings of seven larger-than-
human bronze gourds each etched with tracks of snakes, a shake
of grass, the press of nautilus shells. He calls for sketches of patterns
that praise creatures from the seven continents—worms to weevils,
toads to trout, auks to night herons, snails to cave rats, tigers to
petrels. Impressions of Bennett's algae and African blackwood
leaves. His Gourd Work artisans apply these designs to the lead-free
recycled bronze alloy shells.

The man on the mountain asks people he considers wise what
should rest inside the gourds. North Pacific gyre scientists
contribute frayed rope and the tooth of a narwhal. The DVD of a
Shinto priest grooming a Zen garden. Recordings of meadowlarks.
Archival soundtracks from the Library of Loss. A sculpture of a
golden toad. A Zuni fetish carver offers one carving of as many
extinct or endangered animals as he and his daughter can carve
in one year, made out of jet, the pressured mineral of coal. They
start with a hand-sized black rhino, then the quagga inlaid with
turquoise, an albatross of white marble. A collector donates a claw
of a mute Tasmanian tiger. Birders send feathers. Botanists send
heritage seeds. A vial of run-off from Glacier Park. A canister of
air from 2010. To preserve memories one creature, one habitat at
a time.

People whose ancestors have lived on each continent for millennia choose wind-blown, roadless sacred places for Seven Gourds installations. Each contributor and ecologist, even the rich man on the mountain, says not that the Works are good, but that they are as good as they can do.

American Chestnut

Winter's hunger moon rises before I expect it.
A woman I know died. I mourn a hole, a shadow.
Remember a voice. Arched eyebrows. Her whimsy tied
to what she fashioned with her hands. Shared nieces
and birth years. She is gone.

A maple tree falls. I see its hole, miss a shadow.
I touch its great age—textured, twisted years it knew
before I was born. Four men cut limbs into chunks, haul
and stack as firewood. The trunk does its corpse pose,
their saws not big enough to sunder heartwood.

I cannot imagine the absence chestnuts left,
gone from imported fungus. Four billion dying
in fifty years, this keystone of the forest universe,
what held the arch together—deer, bear,
first people, log cabins where eagles nested.

What the moon knew of its canopies, I never knew.
This hub of a great wheel so vast we could not hold it.
What a forest remembers leaves me mute.
Four sapling chestnuts planted on my land. If we ask
if it's fair to bring a child into this hurt world, what

of those trees, my young chestnuts? Is it smart to clock
their seasons, leaf fall, sprout, leaf fall, sprout,
remnants of ancient turns, what thrived
eons before roasting songs, before blight?
Even when the young die young?

Hope inserts a sliver. We who miss her
remember. Maple body begins its low
weathering into duff. That black chestnut bee,
once thought extinct, survives!—a surprise,
to seek new chestnut flowers from old memory.

Self-Portraits

I painted a self-portrait once. What came out
featured drab daylight and a woman in a black
dress on a hillside, known as female by breasts
and her dress. One tree without leaves. A far-off
stream that seemed to be going uphill.

Before that I made up a song, a soothing song
for a baby. The ditty repeats variants of *om*
to flow with the to-and-fro of a rocking chair
and those babble words, *ba* and *da*.
I'm the only one who remembers how it goes.

I might be my gardens, one after another,
dirt moved around and unpotted roots
set free. Roses, daffodils, milkweed,
daisies, and sunflowers. And the trees—
I have planted so many.

I go to my gardens when I don't know who
I am. Not for discovery. For digging in
to a space where self no longer matters.
Where home is root and tendril,
weed-be-gone and hope.

What I assume and hope you will assume
is my song goes with me, but the trees—
golden willow, spruce, fir, apple, pear,
maple, ash—endure longer than my time
to breathe as I have loved to breathe.

Wheels of Change

Thank God, they cannot cut down the clouds!
—Henry David Thoreau

An Airstream nudges me in passing.
Beasts thicken with winter fur, leaves
mat to the road, the candlestick gutters.

We could be tucked away from trucks
in a house of wood or windows
except now we are on the road.

An air horn blast. The heavy timber,
logging's dray. Round-stacked haul
of lost lives.

This flatbed cannot stop fast.
One hand finds my heart
at this curve where the forest is dying.

See the Forest

Stone-blind to wholes, picking away
for the next needed thing at hand
we cannot see, trees

in sunken ships, Cheerios boxes, hammer handles, Haida
spruce root hats, altars, bowsprits, rocking chairs, postcards,
pick-up sticks, tongue depressors, toothpicks, kindling, splinters,
dreidels, butter churns, toilet seats, arrows, school desks, origami
cranes, birdhouses, crucifixes, wooden nickels, baby cribs, fence
posts, toilet seats, Louisville Sluggers, cellos, bowling alleys,
checkers, junk mail, closet doors, pews, shingles, bibles, atlases,
Lincoln logs, jigsaw puzzles, gallows, playing cards, incense,
snowflakes on school house windows, chopsticks, totem poles,
salad bowls, railroad ties, lobster pots, wine barrels, birth
certificates, sleds, guillotines, walnut gunstocks, whirligig ducks,
pencils, toy pelicans, shoe trees, nutcrackers, railroad crossing gates,
gun racks, drum sticks, oak floors, ebony jewelry boxes, grandfather
clocks, price tags, poisons, Christmas greens, picture frames, docks,
decks, matchsticks, marble raceways, rayon, Tsimshian raven rattles,
pitchfork shafts, ping pong paddles, harpsichords, theatrical snow,
postage stamps, report cards, rolling papers, an obituary, the history
of wildfires, wedding-vow scripts, the air we breathe, and millions
of board feet seized to rebuild after ruin.

The logging truck chugs by in the fast lane.
Chains and tube frames secure full-sized firs
to a flat bed. After the passing at noon
of a stretch hearse with headlights on,
you remember.

Sequester

From Old Latin, meaning "commit to safekeeping"

Where ghosts walk, some mumble *told-you-so.*
They skirt the dog shit, the plastic straws
stuck against park benches. They are tired
of trying to mobilize a union for the dead, find

a sign to wave, or insist someone scrub lichen off
their gravestones. They notice tourists passing by.
They see the black crow take off from crimson
maple branches—the red and black of blood

and despot death. They look beyond the full moon low
and cheesy. Most remember the days when Earth
began to amp up its anger, cycling huge cyclones
and mega-hurricanes, burning or melting north

to release vapors of the old dead, putrid
ones laid to rest with shells, wooden spoons
and furs before they understood a rounded globe
or that heat would become something to fear.

Their footfalls are heard as rodent-like rustles
in these gold leaves tumbling toward equinox
—or sensed like redundant mini-memoirs
about rigid fathers or when-I-was-a-child

we ran wild in the woods and trampled paths
before we ran out of riches to bury people
in forever wood boxes and metal. We say
Someday it won't be the same

as it was, just different, so the leaf song
the children learn in early grades recites
names like juniper, red alder, paper birch,
red oak and ponderosa pine, perhaps resilient,

while older ones learn the word *sequester*
as repair for the damage by our ancestors,
how the ghosts shuffle through yesterdays,
amazed to find how much has changed.

Notes on One Bent Twig

Sentient beings are numberless; I vow to save them.
—One of the Four Great Vows of Zen Buddhism

I was a baby who grew up next to an elm tree
my father planted to shade my bedroom window.

I was a little girl who played at having kitchens
in a woods now given over to a McMansion.

In eighth grade I was taught to sew an apron,
not how to use a lathe to make a salad bowl.

Red oaks we tagged as home base for hide-and-seek
wrote time-lapse cursive on green tornado skies.

No one ever wanted to lynch me
or whip me with a switch.

I've ridden horseback through gold aspen forests
and hiked the timberline of a dormant volcano,

breathed the air sequoias cleanse, and touched
ancient Sitka Spruce in the Hoh River valley.

I am more at ease in a forest than at a cocktail party.
I talk to trees as sisters.

For me, trees frame winter's constellations
and measure the depth of spring's river fogs.

Now the diameter of logs hauled to sawmills
is half what it was forty years ago.

While I am not sure I believe in fairies,
I trust tree spirits to sense my good will.

I have planted forty-five trees, with hope
that each wears its crown in a grace

that orchards planted for rescuers, the Bodhi,
guardian and witness trees have earned.

Monarchs follow a loop to the oyamel firs
tethered to something we do not know.

Great change is upon us. Orchardists know.
So do Port Orford cedars and Florida yews.

Will landscapes of salt cedars, Russian olives,
and Callery pears preach survival stories

as kids turn picture-book pages of old-growth
or visit single survivors of a clan

in tree museums for mountain ash, the totara
of Maori war canoes, and totem poles?

Those children will die
before the end

of the two-hundred thousand
tomorrows that begin to grow a Titan.

Notes on Quotations

Opening epigraphs: The quote from Robin Wall Kimmerer is from *Braiding Sweetgrass: Indigenous Wisdom, Scientific Knowledge and the Teaching of Plants* (Milkweed Editions, 2020). Jack Kerouac's statement is from *The Scripture of the Golden Eternity* (Corinth Books, 1960).

The opening line in "Birch Bark" is from *Thoreau and the Language of Trees* (University of California Press, 2017).

The opening lines of "Additions to the Understory" are from Gary Snyder's poem "For the Children" from *Turtle Island* (New Directions, 1974).

The Joy Harjo line in "Ready to Walk" is from her poem "Speaking Tree" in *Conflict Resolution for Holy Beings* (W. W. Norton, 2015).

The Ursula K. Le Guin line in "Galloping Hooves" is from her poem "Kitchen Spoons" in *Late in the Day: Poems 2010-2014* (PM Press, 2016).

The title of the poem "The Tree of Long Life Is Kindling" refers to a line from Li Po's "Old Dust" as translated by Sam Hamill in *The Poetry of Zen* (Shambhala, 2007).

The Henry David Thoreau quotation about cutting down the clouds was taken from *American Forests'* online journal of Summer 2015.

The Four Vows, variously translated, are widely found on the Internet. This version of the first vow, quoted in the poem "Notes on One Bent Twig," is from the website of New York Zen Center for Contemplative Care.

Acknowledgments

Barrow Street Review: "The Seven Gourd Works Project"
Cirque Journal—A Literary Journal for the North Pacific Rim: "Windfire Smoke from the North"
Cold Mountain Review: "Anthology of Stories Told Over Dinner"
Elohi Gadugi: "Tree Ghosts"
Feminine Collective: "Stripes"
Glint Journal: "California Sycamore"
Highland Park Poetry Gallery: "I Want to Write"
ISLE: Interdisciplinary Studies in Literature and Environment: "Tree Frogs of North Ash Creek"
Kosmos Quarterly: "Tree Sentiency in Six Thousand Languages"
Lines + Stars: "Nurse Log"
Muse/A Journal: "Tenpenny Hammered"
Paddock Review: "The Fig Tree"
Panoplyzine: "My Faith"
Peacock Journal: "The Witness of Rings"
Poemeleon: "The Crowhurst Yew"
The Poeming Pigeon: "Open Spaces on the Universe's Altar"
Sheila-Na-Gig: "Birch Bark," "Name the Dread"
Sliver of Stone: "The Tale End of the Monsoon after Reading Hanshan"
Up the Staircase Quarterly: "Walking into the Shadows of Ashford Forest"
Verse Virtual: "All I Am," "I Looked for a Harbinger," "I Want to Write"
Visitant: "How to Bless," "My Bonsai Tree on the Southern Window Ledge in the Laundry Room"
Woven Tale Press: "My Walk-In Museum of Natural History"

"Galloping Horses" appeared in *Climbing Lightly Through Forests: A Poetry Anthology Honoring Ursula K. Le Guin* (Aqueduct Press, 2021).

"Six Chanticleer Pears on NE 27th" appeared in *Uprooted: An Anthology on Gender and Illness* (Obdurate Oaks Press, 2016).

"Through Flames in the New Year's Fire" appeared in *Four Seasons* (Kind of a Hurricane Press, 2015).

About FutureCycle Press

FutureCycle Press is dedicated to publishing lasting English-language poetry in both print-on-demand and Kindle formats. Founded in 2007 by long-time independent editor/publishers and partners Diane Kistner and Robert S. King, the press was incorporated as a nonprofit in 2012. A number of our editors are distinguished poets and writers in their own right, and we have been actively involved in the small press movement going back to the early seventies.

Each year, we award the FutureCycle Poetry Book Prize and honorarium for the best original full-length volume of poetry we published that year. Introduced in 2013, proceeds from our Good Works projects are donated to charity. Our Selected Poems series highlights contemporary poets with a substantial body of work to their credit; with this series we strive to resurrect work that has had limited distribution and is now out of print.

We are dedicated to giving all of the authors we publish the care their work deserves, offering a catalog of the most diverse and distinguished work possible, and paying forward any earnings to fund more great books. All of our books are kept "alive" and available unless and until an author requests a title be taken out of print.

We've learned a few things about independent publishing over the years. We've also evolved a unique and resilient publishing model that allows us to focus mainly on vetting and preserving for posterity poetry collections of exceptional quality without becoming overwhelmed with bookkeeping and mailing, fundraising activities, or taxing editorial and production "bubbles." To find out more, come see us at futurecycle.org.

The FutureCycle Poetry Book Prize

All original, full-length poetry books published by FutureCycle Press in a given calendar year are considered for the annual FutureCycle Poetry Book Prize. This allows us to consider each submission on its own merits, outside of the context of a traditional contest. Too, the judges see the finished book, which will have benefitted from the beautiful book design and strong editorial gloss we are famous for.

The book ranked the best in judging is announced as the prize-winner in January of the subsequent year. There is no fixed monetary award; instead, the winning poet receives an honorarium of 20% of the total net royalties from all poetry books and chapbooks the press sold online in the year the winning book was published. The winner is also accorded the honor of being on the panel of judges for the next year's competition; judges receive copies of the contending books to keep for their personal library.

Made in the USA
Monee, IL
20 July 2023

39285167R00046